HOPE FOR
Today's Families

WILLIE & ELAINE OLIVER

REVIEW AND HERALD® PUBLISHING ASSOCIATION
Since 1861 | www.reviewandherald.com

Copyright © 2018 by Review and Herald® Publishing Association

Published by Review and Herald® Publishing Association
Printed by Pacific Press® Publishing Association
Printed in the United States of America
All rights reserved

Cover design by Gerald Lee Monks
Cover design resources from iStockphoto.com: FatCamera,
    Geber86, and monkeybusinessimages
Inside design by Kristin Hansen-Mellish

The authors assume full responsibility for the accuracy of all facts
and quotations as cited in this book.

Unless otherwise noted, all Bible quotations are from the New
King James Version. Copyright © 1979, 1980, 1982 by Thomas
Nelson, Inc. Used by permission. All rights reserved.

Scripture quotations marked ESV are from *The Holy Bible,* English
Standard Version, copyright © 2001 by Crossway, a publishing
ministry of Good News Publishers. Used by permission. All rights
reserved.

Scripture quotations marked NIV are from the *Holy Bible, New
International Version*. Copyright © 1973, 1978, 1984, 2011 by
Biblica, Inc. Used by permission. All rights reserved worldwide.

You can obtain additional copies of this book by calling toll-free
1-800-765-6955 or by visiting http://www.adventistbookcenter.com.

ISBN: 978-0-8280-2830-1

November 2018

Table of Contents

Introduction

Developing a healthy family is among the most challenging tasks human beings can undertake. Even when people are intentional about having healthy relationships in their families, it is still challenging—despite our best intentions—because we are all human, and every human being is imperfect. Our failings make it very difficult to sustain healthy relationships.

However, there *is* hope for today's families. Things can get better. Our children can grow up and become positive and vibrant human beings. We can learn to overcome negative attitudes. As you embrace God's reasons for creating the family, it is possible to have stronger and healthier family relationships.

One of the important dynamics in healthy families is the quality of their communication. Good communication in a two-parent family is not much different from good communication in a single-parent home. Any meaningful and relevant conversation about families will need to address the common struggles that are often found in families around the world.

Relationships in families vary based on the people who make up that particular family. There is no cookie-cutter way of handling families. The interactions among people who live with three or four generations under the same roof will be a little different from those of a household that is limited to parents and their underage children. However, as we have already mentioned, the standard principles of good family relations—in many ways—are universal.

From Addis Ababa to Adelaide; from Bali to Buenos Aires; from Cape Town to Chicago; from Dewas to Detroit; from Eldoret to Ensenada; from Florence to Fortaleza; from Gaborone to Geneva; from Haifa to Hanoi; from Istanbul to Ibadan; from Jerusalem to Juba; from Kuala Lumpur to Kabul; from Los Angeles to Lahore; from Madrid to Mumbai; from New York City to Nairobi; from Orlando to Osaka; from Port Moresby to Panama City; from Quito to

Quezon City; from Riga to Rio de Janeiro; from San Salvador to Shanghai; from Tegucigalpa to Timisoara; from Ulaanbaatar to Uppsala; from Volgograd to Valparaíso; from Washington, DC, to Warsaw; from Xi'an to Xalapa; from York to Yaoundé; from Zanzibar City to Zaragoza; several basic skills are available to enhance and improve family relationships in villages and cities around the world.

In this little book, we plan to share several essential areas for successful family relations. Regardless of whether you are single, married, divorced, never married, with children or without them, younger or older, we hope you will find tools in these pages that can transform all your relationships from just tolerable to magnificent.

In chapter 1, we talk about the family as God's invention from the very beginning of time, why it is so important, and the many roles it plays in our lives to give us a sense of self and the stability we need to get through life.

In chapter 2, we share about marriage the way God intended it to be and the need to focus more on what you can give, rather than what you can get. We also share an important metaphor that will help you easily visualize how you can get the most out of marriage by investing in your marriage every day.

In chapter 3, we reveal the secrets of parenting

for success. Raising children today is more challenging than ever. And shaping a child's character is even more urgent as children are confronted daily with values that seem opposite of their parents' values—bombarded with mixed messages from social media and many other sources. If you want to be better prepared to tackle this tremendous challenge, you must read this chapter.

In chapter 4, we communicate the importance of understanding that obedience is for everyone who wants to be successful in relationships. Unless we come to grips with the principles God left in place to help us develop important values that facilitate peace and happiness in all of our relationships, life will continue to be less than what God intended for it to be.

In chapter 5, we write about how husbands and wives can become intimate allies. We warn that every marriage will naturally move toward a state of isolation unless the partners are intentional every day about developing closeness with each other through the power of God. Married people who are intimate emotionally, financially, spiritually, and intellectually tend to support each other when faced with a challenge from an outside force or person.

In chapter 6, we deal with the importance of communicating with grace in all of your relationships. As human beings, we all make mistakes. By approaching the activity of communication with grace, you will be able to communicate within a framework that facilitates closeness and growth.

In chapter 7, we share priceless information about the destructive nature of violence and abuse in the family and review God's original intent and perfect plan for our relationships and families.

In chapter 8, we disclose scientific evidence for how to prevent marital distress and divorce so that your marriage can be a place of growth, contentment, and peace. If you are married or thinking about being married in the near future, you cannot afford to miss this discussion.

In chapter 9, we address the social processes affecting single people and the importance of finding peace with yourself and your circumstances if you are single. We also deal with the reality that many single adults wish they could be married and believe their lives would be easier to manage and live responsibly if this was their reality. Is this really true? Do married people have an advantage in this world that we inhabit? We look at how to find greater peace in your life as a single person.

In the afterword, we integrate the messages of each chapter, as pieces of a puzzle that when brought together share a picture of the hope God has for every family relationship.

Having a relatively healthy family is a gift from

God. To be sure, it takes effort, intentionality, and reliance on the Almighty. Nevertheless, you should always remember that God has promised to be with you until the end of the age (Matthew 28:20); to give you His peace (John 14:27); and to supply all of your needs (Philippians 4:19). Let's trust Him despite the challenges faced each day of our lives and embrace the fact that there is hope for today's families.

1

The Family: God's Invention

Family is a wonderful word that stirs up warm feelings in most people around the world. It is the first thing people think about when in danger and also when there is something good to share or celebrate. Family is the first thing in our thoughts after being away for school or work for a period. Most people think about wanting to hug loved ones and enjoy the familiar surroundings of home after being away for some time. The truth is that, after God, family is consistently the most significant group that makes us feel safe, secure, and warm.

The experience of family did not happen by chance. Family was God's plan for the human race from the very beginning of time. It is the group from which we get our identity, our name, and our traditions. Family are the people we have a long-term relationship with, and, frequently, we feel the most comfortable with them. Family is almost always where we get the inner driving force that influences our goals and aspirations, and even our sense of well-being—who we really are or who we want to become.

When we think of family, we reflect on our parents, brothers and sisters, grandparents, aunts, uncles, cousins, spouse, and children. Sometimes we even consider good friends to be family, because

- we grew up together in the same church or neighborhood;
- we are from the same city or country;
- we belong to the same tribe or region;
- we adopted each other or connected in some special way; or
- we share similar values, goals, or affinities.

What may come to mind when we think of family are our memories of faces, shapes, smells, or conversations; private and public spaces; a house or apartment; a city or a suburb; a farm or a village; a church or a school; a kitchen and food.

Genesis 1:27, 28 describes the beginnings of the family like this: "So God created man in His own image; in the image of God He created him; male and female He created them. Then God blessed them, and God said to them, 'Be fruitful and multiply; fill the earth and subdue it.' "

The Bible—the inspired literature that describes God's conversation with human beings— shares in the first chapter of the first book that God created the family, emphasizing the high importance this basic unit in society has for God, and consequently should have for us.

Despite God's plan for the happiness of the family, we all know things have not always worked as well as they were supposed to. Husbands and wives often do not get along. The marriage that was meant to last until death often ends in divorce—or the relationship doesn't even get to marriage before giving birth to children, separating, and causing lots of pain. Parents and children are often angry at each other. Parents feel disrespected, while children feel controlled or abandoned by the ones who were supposed to be taking care of them.

These experiences are often confusing because what we anticipated would bring a sense of happiness, warm feelings, and security has been the complete opposite for many people in our world today, perhaps even for the person reading this book right now.

In the face of disappointment and distress we are pleased to share that there is hope for today's family. Left to the popular attitudes in our society of thinking about ourselves first, second, and always—what can I get, rather than what can I give—families will continue to experience anguish, depression, gloom, hopelessness, and misery. The hope is in taking another look at the principles God meant for people to follow so that their families could be what He created them to be. Beyond just taking a look, putting these principles into practice enables us to experience the joy, warmth, and peace that family was designed to bring.

So how would you describe your family relationships? Is there peace and a sense of satisfaction in your home each day, or does your family life feel more like a street fight you are trying to get away from or simply attempting to survive every day? Do you think you are making progress in your quest for developing a stronger and healthier family, or are you feeling angry, frustrated, irritated, and more helpless with every passing day?

What can be done to improve your relationships from apparent failure to working relationships where family members truly communicate?

Glad you asked. The truth is that there are no perfect families because there are no perfect people. So when we talk about a family that feels connected, we are not talking about a family without any problems. Rather, we are describing a family that enjoys relatively high levels of satisfaction and stability among its members. A family that is connected in a healthy way—spouses, parents, and children—are intentional about managing conflict in a timely manner and are committed to being patient, kind, understanding, and forgiving. While this kind of commitment is not easy, it is worthwhile and will contribute to the happiness, health, and quality of life of every family who puts it into practice.

For families to make it through the years with a high probability of success, it is important for family members to be committed to making it through each day—one at a time. Every member of the family must be purposeful about getting along with each other in meaningful ways every day—listening to each other, practicing being patient with each other when doing the opposite is so much easier because it comes naturally.

These are the habits that, if practiced daily, build stronger and healthier families over the years and make the members of the family feel safe, cared for, and secure, making it so much easier to deal with the difficulties that will inevitably be experienced by every family. This kind of family relationship is better than any insurance policy when it comes to protecting a family from unexpected events.

Family specialists often say that the quality of a family depends on the quality of their communication. Trying to grow a strong family relationship without healthy communication is like attempting to make grape juice without grapes. It is simply impossible. Healthy communication is the primary skill needed for maintaining a strong sense of family. The closer the family relationship becomes, the more caring and respectful the communication must be.

Stephen R. Covey, a leading family expert, shares in his book *The 7 Habits of Highly Effective Families,*[1] the concept "be proactive" as a skill to be used for effective communication. In essence, the idea indicates that between a stimulus and the response—what someone says to you, and how you respond—there is a space. And in that space each family member has the freedom and power to choose their response—what they say, and how they say it. And that response is truly at the foundation of their growth and happiness as a family. For this concept to work so a family is able to communicate effectively, however, the skill has to be practiced so that it can be learned. To be sure, three things *must* happen in the space

between what a family member says to you and
how you respond:

1. You must *pause*—instead of responding
   immediately to what your father or mother,
   daughter or son, husband or wife, is saying,
   allow yourself to calm down.
2. You must then *think* about what you should
   or should not say.
3. You must *choose* the correct response: what
   will bring peace, rather than war, to the situation at hand.

The quality of your family life will have much
to do with the quality of your communication.
Families who speak with each other regularly and
lovingly experience a level of closeness that families
who rarely or unkindly communicate with each
other can never achieve.

It takes determination to build a great family.
But anything that is worth doing is worth doing
well. So make the commitment to communicate
well, and watch your family blossom and grow in
the days, weeks, months, and years ahead.

———————
1. Stephen R. Covey, *The 7 Habits of Highly Effective Families* (New York: Golden Books, 1997).

2

Marriage God's Way

To celebrate our thirtieth marriage anniversary and create new memories to keep our marriage healthy and strong, we spent five days at the beach, enjoying the beautiful sand and clear blue water.

Our time at the beach was simply wonderful. We relaxed, read books, enjoyed good food, swam, snorkeled, and went bodyboarding and kayaking; but the most unforgettable of all our activities was learning to sail.

As our sailing lesson began, we quickly realized there was much more difficulty to this sport than one could see on the surface. While a bit stressful, it was also relaxing, challenging, and rewarding. In our sailing lesson it soon became obvious that we would need to work together as a team and be on the same side of the sailboat to experience gliding smoothly across the beautiful Caribbean waters.

God created marriage and family to give human beings the needed community to feel connected. While the process has challenging moments, the rewards are out of this world.

The Bible is full of good counsel to help us negotiate our family relationships for maximum joy. The more we read the Word of God ourselves and with our spouse, the more we will be in tune with what God wants for us and for our families. The truth is, it is impossible as humans always to protect love from harm or hurt. However, as we apply God's Word to our family relationships, we can find the capacity to honor God in our relationships. This can take place, however, only as we make the time to be with each other and grow together through the power of God.

We love to spend time together—just the two of us. Now that we've been married for more than thirty years and have had the privilege of working together, we have all kinds of favorite activities and places to visit. We are simply grateful that God brought us together, and we try to apply the counsel we find in the Bible to our marriage relationship every day. One of our favorite verses that we like to apply to our communication with each other is found in James 1:19, which says: "Everyone should be quick to listen, slow to speak and slow to become angry" (NIV).

Working closely together, as we do, is gratifying but also challenging. We choose to schedule fun times together and to find reasons to celebrate often to keep our marriage and family a desirable place to be. After working for several days on completing work projects, one of our favorite things to do is to find a good Indian restaurant and share a meal together. While we try to be careful not to overeat, we enjoy food and find it a reason to celebrate God and life during a great meal of chana masala, baigan bharta, dal makhani, rice, and tandoori roti. And, if we have been faithful to our weekly exercise program, we may add a glass of mango lassi to complete the experience.

Our children are grown and no longer live at home. However, every time we get a chance to be together, we spend time visiting and enjoying our family. Whether playing a game, sharing a favorite meal, visiting a museum, or going to church together, we are reminded that we belong to each other and are grateful to God for His goodness to us. When we are apart, we stay connected by keeping in touch on a regular basis. Of course, we can make this happen only by thinking and planning for it. But it is a worthwhile investment for the health and strength of our marriage and family.

God's plan for marriage is more easily fulfilled when married couples use a concept called *the emotional bank account.* The emotional bank account is like any other bank account. You can make withdrawals from an account only when it has funds in it. And we all know what happens when we make more withdrawals than deposits from our bank accounts. We end up with insufficient funds when we write a check from that account.

The same is true of your marriage relationship. If all you do in your marriage is take, take, and take, without contributing to the well-being of your spouse first, you can't expect to get anything out of your marriage relationship. When you are kind to your spouse, you are making deposits in their emotional bank account. The more emotional deposits you make in the emotional bank account of your spouse, the *richer* your relationship will be. The reverse—trying to get more than you give—leads to a bankrupt relationship.

So how are you doing with deposits in the emotional bank account of your spouse? Are you kind, patient, supportive, encouraging, and forgiving on a regular basis? Or are you cynical, impatient, critical, demanding, difficult, and offensive?

Regardless of how difficult your marriage relationship has been, you can turn things around if you make up your mind to begin doing things differently. Rather than approaching your marriage from the angle of what you can get, start looking at your marriage from the perspective of what you can give. Then watch your spouse's emotional bank account grow and grow until your relationship is bursting with the currency of goodwill for each other.

The following six behaviors can help any couple get their marriage's emotional bank account back on track. Couples who are willing to try at least one of these suggestions will most likely see improvement in their relationship immediately:

Stop labeling your marriage as dysfunctional!

The human brain is wired to believe what we tell it. If you keep saying your marriage is dysfunctional, you will begin to believe it. We like to tell people to ask themselves, "Do I have a good marriage with some dysfunctional times, or do I have a lousy marriage with a few good times?" It's a case of the proverbial, "Is the glass half full or half empty?" Couples who are willing to find the good in their marriage and in their spouse will be able to more easily resolve conflict and have a more satisfying marriage. So start telling yourself that you have a great marriage, and you and your spouse will begin to believe it.

The truth is, any marriage can be turned around if the couple believes in it and is willing to commit to making their marriage grow stronger. God's Word is true when it declares, "If you can believe, all things are possible to him who believes" (Mark 9:23).

Pray with all your heart for your marriage and your spouse

God, the Creator, invented marriage. Therefore, it is not only wise but also essential to keep Him at the center of your marriage. We don't mean just paying lip service to this; we mean establishing and maintaining a meaningful relationship with God and constantly acknowledging His presence as individuals, and also as a couple. Ask God to heal your marriage, and then expect a miracle. God "is able to do exceedingly abundantly above all that we ask or think, according to the power that works in us" (Ephesians 3:20). We also tell couples if they believed God is present while they are speaking to one another, would they really say some of the things they say to each other? Or would they be more inclined to impress God with how kind, patient, loving, and forgiving they are? Especially as you ask God every day to forgive you for your sins and to favor you with His grace and mercy, how can you do less for your spouse? God promises that if we humbly seek Him when we pray, he will hear us, forgive us, and heal our brokenness (2 Chronicles 7:14).

Learn and practice effective communication skills

This may seem really obvious and instinctive. But, the truth is, this is not inborn or easy at all. While we have all learned to communicate since birth, most of us have developed flawed or incorrect methods of communication. We learn how to communicate in our families of origin, and we bring those patterns—good and bad— into our marriage. In addition, what worked well in our homes or with our friends may not work in our marriage, with our spouse. Each partner needs to be willing to make adjustments in their own relational and communication styles in ways that can enhance the quality of the relationship. Most disagreements happen in marriage because couples are talking over each other and neither partner has stopped to listen to the needs, wants, and hurts of their spouse.

A fair number of problems in marriage are not really problems. Many issues can be resolved by taking the time to listen to each other and to seek genuine understanding. We are back to the wisdom found in James 1:19, about being quick to listen, slow to speak, and slow to be angry.

Find out what your spouse likes and do it, and keep doing it—and find out what your spouse doesn't like and quit doing it!

Prior to marriage couples take great care in being their best selves—the best boyfriend or the best girlfriend. They go out of their way to find out what the other person likes, to shower them with their heart's desires. After the wedding and the honeymoon period, however, they think they no longer need to do special things for each other. Of course, this change makes your spouse feel taken for granted. This is when you hear people say they married the wrong person. It isn't so much that they married the wrong person. Rather, each one just stopped being the right person. To make matters worse, they begin to irritate each other by doing the very things they know their spouse dislikes.

If couples would employ the golden rule of Matthew 7:12, "so whatever you wish that others would do to you, do also to them" (ESV), they would literally watch their marriages flourish and grow exponentially.

Forgive often
In marriage—the most intimate relationship—couples will experience hurt[1] from time to time.

Thus, couples will need to learn to forgive each other. Sometimes one partner hurts the other unintentionally. There are also times when people wound each other by saying offensive and nasty things to retaliate for pain they may be experiencing. Some injuries can be easily ignored, some are a little harder to forgive, and others leave deep and lasting scars.

Forgiving someone who has harmed you is the hardest part of loving, and yet you cannot continue to truly love without doing it. Forgiveness is not about becoming a doormat to be trampled upon, absolving others from responsibility, or simply forgetting. Still, forgiving actually helps begin the process of healing from your hurts and from the need to punish the other person. It also pushes you toward restoring the fracture in the relationship. And, through God's power, you will be able to give the gift of forgiveness to your spouse. Romans 5:8 offers, "God shows his love for us in that while we were still sinners, Christ died for us" (ESV).

Laugh a lot

The old adage "Laughter is good medicine" still rings true today. In fact, medical research has found that laughter has physiological and neurological benefits. Laughter helps reduce stress, stimulates the immune system, reduces blood pressure, bonds couples together, and keeps the relationship fresh. We tell couples to find things to laugh about and stop stressing about the small stuff. Again, many issues couples have in marriage are simply idiosyncrasies. Nevertheless, they, too, can learn to laugh at unintended misunderstandings. Proverbs 17:22 shares, "A merry heart does good, like medicine, but a broken spirit dries the bones."

Conclusion

Marriage is at once awesome, wonderful, and difficult. Awesome and wonderful because it was designed by the Creator for us to reflect His image. Difficult because it brings together two flawed, imperfect, selfish human beings who become even more flawed and selfish once married. Married couples need to confront this reality and work together as teammates and friends. Together, we must fight the enemy that threatens to destroy our oneness with each other and our oneness with God.

---

1. We are not talking about the pain of abuse. If you are experiencing any type of physical or emotional abuse in your relationship, please seek help from a qualified counselor or pastor. Without help, the abuse will most likely get worse. For more information, visit Adventist Family Ministries at http://www.family.adventist.org.

3

Parenting for Success

Raising children today is more challenging than ever. Shaping a child's character is even more urgent as children are confronted daily with values that seem opposite from their parents' values. Today children are bombarded with mixed messages through the media, internet, other adults, and their peers. These confusing messages have led children down a path that desensitizes them to many societal ills such as violence, immorality, abuse, and discrimination.

The statistics on teen homicide, bullying in schools, school shootings, suicides, and drug and alcohol abuse reflect significant changes to the nature of childhood. Thus, it is much harder for children to learn basic lessons of self-management, self-esteem, and empathy toward others. Children today are more prone to depression, anxiety, and impulsive behavior. At the same time, there are more economic pressures on parents, who are working harder and longer hours, leaving them less time to spend with their children.

In spite of these challenges, parents are still the best protection against children participating in risky behaviors such as drug and alcohol use, premarital sex, and eating disorders. Parents who daily take an active role in raising their children will eventually reap the rewards of seeing their children grow into healthy and responsible adults. While parenting is not an exact science and there are no guarantees, parents who make the most of their time with their children will be more likely to influence them and prepare them for adulthood.

There are times when parenting seems like an insignificant task, especially when one is changing diapers, wiping up spills, or arguing about curfews and dirty rooms. However, parenting is one of the most important and challenging tasks given to human beings. Consider the significance of raising a child who will not just be obedient but will grow to have a mature character and a healthy self-esteem, manage their emotions, and have healthy relationships with others. Parenting is of the utmost importance.

Of course, there is no such thing as a perfect parent. However, by God's grace our children may grow up to be fine adults, despite having had parents who were less than perfect. On the same note, parents should not expect their children to be perfect either. In the rest of this chapter, we share some ways in which parents can lay a solid foundation to carry out the task of raising their children successfully.

We said earlier that while there are no guarantees in parenting, parents can do things to increase the probability of being successful in this important work. Since raising children to have mature characters and to be responsible adults in society is the primary goal of parenting, it is important for parents to understand what their values are and how to transmit them into their children's character.

Let's begin with an understanding of what *values* are. Values are important beliefs shared by the members of a culture or family about what is good and what is not. Values wield major influence on the behavior of an individual and serve as rules or guidelines in all situations. Some fundamental moral values are honesty, integrity, respect, and responsibility for others.

The character is how values are activated.

Character is not what we say—it is who we are. It is how we live out our values. So, if you tell a child that honesty is an important value in your home but you then tell her to tell the person who has just called on the phone that you are not home when you are obviously at home, your child will internalize that honesty is not an important value. Character is observable in a person's behavior. Remember, values are our beliefs, while character is active.

Character is made up of foundational values we mentioned earlier—honesty, respect, kindness, empathy, and responsibility. When these qualities are part of a person's character, one can expect to witness them regularly and consistently in the person's behavior. When these values become a part of a child's character, you would not expect them to change as the child interacts with different people or in different situations.

Again, because no one is perfect, there will be times your child may not exhibit these traits of character. However, the more the preferred values are reinforced, the more they will become a part of your child. Hence, parents must also strive to live by these values. On that point, someone once said that your child may not do what you say; they are more likely to do what they see you do.

The term *emotional intelligence* has become one of the most popular phrases of the new millennium. In fact, psychologists have found that emotional intelligence, or EQ, is a better predictor of a person's success in life than IQ. They have discovered that EQ leads to happiness in all aspects of life—work, career, and relationships. So, what is emotional intelligence, or EQ? EQ is the ability to control one's emotions. It is being aware of your emotions and having the ability to manage these emotions even in the most stressful of situations.

Dr. John Gottman, a leading psychologist who has done extensive research in marriage and parenting, suggests that parents need to become involved with their children's feelings. Parents must become emotion coaches. Parents should use negative and positive emotions as opportunities to teach their children important lessons about life and build a closer relationship with them. Dr. Gottman is clear that emotion coaching does not mean that parents should do away with discipline but helps parents have more successful parent-child interactions.[1]

Parents can become emotion coaches for their children by following these steps:

1. Become aware of your child's emotions. All emotions are an opportunity for a closer relationship with your child and for teaching.
2. Listen sincerely to your child. Parents must learn to listen to their children and validate their feelings. Your attitude toward your

children is essential in helping them become emotionally intelligent and responsible adults. Make sure that your language is not critical, judgmental, or blaming.

3. Help your children find ways to label the emotions they are feeling. Sometimes your child may yell, hit, or stomp, and this is normally interpreted as anger. However, most times these fits of anger are just expressions of what your child is really feeling. Instead of getting angry at your child and yelling and screaming, ask the child what he or she is feeling and provide feeling words such as *sad, frustrated, embarrassed, shy, upset.*

4. Set limits while exploring solutions to the problem at hand. Children need parents to set clear limits that are age appropriate. Children rely on this guidance in both childhood and adolescence. Children begin asking for independence from very early on; however, the parent who gives independence without limits is not doing the child a favor. Rather, this creates havoc and insecurity for the child. On the other hand, a parent who is too controlling and does not allow a child to exercise some independence hinders the child's development. Children must be respected, acknowledged as having a point of view, and given opportunities to make choices.

Knowing about values, character, and emotional intelligence is one thing, but how do parents help children move from thinking to doing? How do we help our children turn nouns such as *generosity, kindness, thoughtfulness, sensitivity, forgiveness,* and *compassion* into action verbs? Children do not acquire emotional intelligence or good character by memorization of rules and regulations. A list of good qualities and virtues will be as quickly forgotten as they are memorized; but when children get to practice what they have learned, the concepts become a part of them. As values are internalized, being *good* becomes a part of your child's identity.

To parent for success, parents must understand several truisms and apply them to their relationship with their child or children. As parents, you must first and foremost understand that respect is at the core of morality—respect for self, for others, and for the Creator of the universe. As a parent, you must respect your children and expect them to respect you in return. If you want to raise responsible children who have your values, you must treat them as human beings.

Parents, remember that actions speak louder than words. Children observe everything their parents do. They file it away and later imitate how the significant adults in their lives live, what they do, and how they treat those around them. Modeling is a very effective teacher. But remember, modeling is not about perfection. It *is* about letting your children see your commitment to moral ideals or Christian ideals. It is also about modeling what moral people do when they have made a mistake. It is saying you are sorry. It is about talking to your children about your struggles to *live* the way you *believe*. If you are a Christian and you believe in Christ, it is essential for you to show your children how to live like Christ did when He walked on this earth.

Parents must let their values be seen and heard. As the old saying puts it, "We must not only practice what we preach but preach what we practice." Children need our words as well as our actions. For maximum impact, not only must they be taught the values, but they need to know the reasons and beliefs that lie behind them. Parents need to guide, instruct, listen, and advise.

Make love the foundation on which you build every aspect of your relationship with your child or children. The New Testament says, "God is love" (1 John 4:16). It is God's love that we reflect to our children. Children need to be rooted and grounded in love, the kind of love that God bestows upon us as unconditional love. The kind of love that does not require anything in return. This kind of love helps our children develop a positive self-concept, a sense of worth, an inner strength. The love that we are speaking about is active, not passive.

In parenting, *love* looks like focused attention, time, support, connectedness, boundaries, and commitment. This genuine, active love bonds you to your child or children. This kind of love teaches children to love themselves and to love others. Children—or adults—who do not feel loved have much difficulty loving themselves, and in turn they have difficulty loving others. Children need to know they are being heard and that they are important enough for you to devote your full attention to what they have to say. This makes them feel loved.

There are no shortcuts in parenting, not even for busy parents. The *quality* of time does not make up for minimal *quantity*. Healthy families structure their schedules, however busy and hectic, to spend time together eating, working, and playing. The bottom line is this: Parenting takes time.

Parents must foster an I-can-do-it attitude by encouraging their children to try new things. You must learn to celebrate successes and reframe *failures* as simply *tries that teach us what does not work*. A child who receives much more praise and appreciation than criticism and blaming will grow to have a positive self-image. Supportive parents help their children to develop a sense of themselves as capable and competent persons who can stand up for what is right and who do not need the approval of the group at any price.

Children who feel supported are less susceptible to negative peer pressure.

To be sure, love and limits go together. These two factors are the most significant predictors of the kind of parenting that produces children most likely to buy into their parents' values and most likely to have the capacity to establish warm, positive relationships with others. Ultimately, children need most of all to know there is nothing they can ever say or do or be that moves them out of the circle of their parents' love.

When parents set the foundation for positive and healthy development in their children's lives, then children will have the best chance of becoming the persons God intends them to be. Your child or children will be able to choose right when faced with tough decisions; they will not be easily swayed by others' opinions. Not only will they find that a strong character coupled with emotional intelligence benefits them personally, but they will also be a benefit to the family, church, and society as a whole because they have been given the essential building blocks for living a healthy life.

---

1. John M. Gottman and Joan DeClaire, *Raising an Emotionally Intelligent Child: The Heart of Parenting* (New York: Fireside, 1998), 27.

4

Rock or Sand?

On a recent trip to Côte d'Ivoire (Ivory Coast) for leadership meetings with our West-Central Africa networks, our flight from Paris to Abidjan was delayed by a couple of hours. Already scheduled to arrive an hour before midnight, the delay meant the driver picking us up from the airport would be having a very long night and early morning.

To make matters worse, instead of making up time—which often happens with many delayed flights—our layover in Ouagadougou, the capital city of Burkina Faso, became a disaster. A passenger who boarded in Paris, headed to Abidjan, could not be found, causing anxiety among the crew and further postponing our arrival in Abidjan. This new reality made us somewhat concerned, wondering whether our driver, whom we did not know and had never met, would still be at the airport when we arrived in the wee hours of the morning.

Thankfully, our story has a happy ending. We are convinced it is because someone poured great values into Charles, our driver. Integrity, honor, and an amazing work ethic were all on display that day.

Charles was at the airport to meet us as though it were the middle of the afternoon. A man with a very kind and pleasant disposition, he drove us safely to our lodging place at three o'clock in the morning. There is no doubt in our minds that Charles's character was built on the foundation provided by his parents or guardians and his own commitment to being obedient to the values he learned as a child.

Jesus, in Matthew 7:24–27, uttered the following in the Sermon on the Mount:

> Everyone then who hears these words of mine and does them will be like a wise man who built his house on the rock. And the rain fell, and the floods came, and the winds

blew and beat on that house, but it did not fall, because it had been founded on the rock. And everyone who hears these words of mine and does not do them will be like a foolish man who built his house on the sand. And the rain fell, and the floods came, and the winds blew and beat against that house, and it fell, and great was the fall of it (ESV).

These words concluded Jesus' discourse on the ethics of the kingdom of God and His expectations for those who would be His followers and all who would choose to live an upstanding life based on eternal values.

The truth is, the same danger still exists today. So many take it for granted that they are good people, even Christians, because they endorse certain spiritual beliefs. But they have not integrated the values found in the teachings of Jesus into their daily lives. And, because they have not truly believed in these fundamental principles for living a life based on good morals, they have not received the power and grace that come through their commitment to doing what God asks them to do to ensure greater happiness in their lives.

Interestingly enough, family life and the Christian life are not much different when observed from a similar vantage point. Knowing what God expects and doing what God requires are two entirely different realities.

In the heart of the Sermon on the Mount, the sacredness of marriage looms large. Matthew 5:27, 28 declares: "You have heard that it was said to those of old, 'You shall not commit adultery.' But I say to you that whoever looks at a woman to lust for her has already committed adultery with her in his heart." The Bible writer further explains the intention of the passage in verse 32 by affirming: "But I say to you that whoever divorces his wife for any reason except sexual immorality causes her to commit adultery; and whoever marries a woman who is divorced commits adultery."

Referencing the currency of every healthy marriage, Paul declares under divine inspiration in 1 Corinthians 13:1–8:

> If I speak in the tongues of men and of angels, but have not love, I am a noisy gong or a clanging cymbal. And if I have prophetic powers, and understand all mysteries and all knowledge, and if I have all faith, so as to remove mountains, but have not love, I am nothing. If I give away all I have, and if I deliver up my body to be burned, but have not love, I gain nothing.
>
> Love is patient and kind; love does not envy or boast; it is not arrogant or rude.

41

It does not insist on its own way; it is not irritable or resentful; it does not rejoice at wrongdoing, but rejoices with the truth. Love bears all things, believes all things, hopes all things, endures all things.

Love never ends (ESV).

Many today have forgotten that marriage was established by God at the very beginning of human history as a divine institution of foremost importance, when He declared in Genesis 2:18, "It is not good that man should be alone; I will make him a helper comparable to him." A few verses later God declared: "Therefore a man shall leave his father and mother and be joined to his wife, and they shall become one flesh" (verse 24).

And lest anyone suggest that this is an Old Testament notion that no longer applies to us today, the New Testament repeats this text three more times, in Matthew 19:5; Mark 10:7, 8; and Ephesians 5:31, to make clear God's intention about marriage as the closest, most intimate relationship humans should have.

These passages in the Bible are filled with irrefutable requirements, including the reality of husband and wife being in the singular rather than the plural form. It is the normative biblical command that marriage was meant to take place between one man and one woman when it says in 1 Corinthians 7:2: "Nevertheless, because of sexual immorality, let each man have his own wife, and let each woman have her own husband." Anything more or less than that is of human origin and does not support the model established by God in Eden. It is certainly difficult to overlook the detail that God's intention was for marriage to be forever.

Undeniably, God created marriage and the family to be a blessing and a joy to human beings. The oneness mentioned in Genesis 2:24 was meant to counteract the loneliness felt by man in Genesis 2:18, 20. This oneness was meant to be a good thing. And yet, everything God created for our good, evil tries to destroy. This evil—fueled by Satan—seems to be succeeding with the help of many husbands and wives who have totally forgotten God's objective for marriage.

As you consider the solid principles of morality and decency evidenced in the wisdom of biblical literature, you must ask yourself whether you are building your marriage and family on the rock or on the sand. If you only talk a good talk but you don't walk the good walk, are you simply fooling yourself and missing out on the joy, peace, and blessings God wants you to have in your marriage and family life?

While we tend to forget that God's design is perfect and was created with our well-being in mind, it is important that we decide for ourselves to go to Him to learn from Him and receive power from Him to live out His plans for our lives. Because every crisis in marriage and family is a spiritual crisis that can be solved only through the power of God. When you put into practice the teachings He has left for you to follow, you are building your marriage and family relationships on a solid foundation, rather than on the sand. We also know that every crisis in marriage and family is an opportunity for growth, and today is your opportunity to grow.

To have a great marriage and family, it is important to have excellent communication in one's relationships. We often miss having great relationships because of habits we have developed in our families of origin. We give ourselves a moral license by saying: "This is who I am; love me or leave me. I am a good person. I volunteer to feed the homeless and contribute to many charities."

Let's go back to the teachings found in the Sermon on the Mount that say: "Everyone then who hears these words of mine and does them will be like a wise man who built his house on the rock" (Matthew 7:24, ESV). So if your marriage and family relationships are not going too well, what can you change about your current behavior so that you can be a blessing to your spouse and family? If you think it is too difficult to change, remember, with God all things are possible, and He will help you if you desire to live a better life in your relationships.

To build your marriage and family relationships on the rock means to put into practice the ethical teachings of Jesus Christ rather than building your family relationships on the sands of your own opinions or those offered by the loose morals of our times.

5

Becoming Intimate Allies

Several years ago, we found a quotation by an unknown author that says: "Getting married is easy. Staying married is more difficult. Staying happily married for a lifetime would be considered among the fine arts."

It really does not take a genius to accept the reality of this statement. If you simply take a good look at the people around you—those you associate with each day—you will quickly realize how true this statement is.

Even if you have been married for only a few months, you have already experienced how challenging it is to stay married, let alone to stay happily married! So how do you develop and maintain an intimate relationship with your spouse, and how do you become allies?

When we reference intimacy here, it is probably not what most of you are thinking about right now. The intimacy we are talking about is simply a closeness that every married couple needs to develop—emotionally, financially, spiritually, and intellectually. While physical intimacy is very important in marriage, if a married couple does not experience the intimacy we are talking about in this piece, they may never truly experience the intimacy needed to go the distance in marriage. A dictionary definition of *intimacy* in marriage we found a long time ago states: "An affectionate bond, the strands of which are composed of mutual caring, responsibility, trust, open communication of feelings and sensations, as well as the non-defended interchange of information about significant events."[1]

A dictionary definition of *ally* is simply "to associate or connect by some mutual relationship, as a resemblance or friendship." Another meaning we found is "to unite formally, as by treaty, league, marriage, or the like."

Hence, this chapter deals with developing a relationship with your spouse that is close and finds you united. Married people who are allied are very close emotionally, financially, spiritually, and intellectually; and they tend to support each other when faced with a challenge from an outside force or person.

Ellen White, a prolific Christian writer of the nineteenth and early twentieth century, stated, "However carefully and wisely marriage may have been entered into, few couples are completely united when the marriage ceremony is performed. The real union of the two in wedlock is the work of the after years."[2]

The truth about marriage is that regardless of how long two people have known each other before getting married or how compatible they seem to be, because we are all sinners and fundamentally selfish our marriage relationship will naturally lead to a state of alienation and separation.

The good news, however, is that husbands and wives can become intimate allies. Our marriages can grow. We have choices. We can learn to live with what is wrong—which ultimately leads to contempt, resentment, and isolation—or we can fight to have a great marriage.

The best choice we can make to become intimate allies is to be intentional about connecting with each other every day through the power of God. Since marriage was God's idea, and He meant for marriage to be a blessing to us, to our families, to our neighborhoods, and to the world, we need to trust Him to give us the desire and the strength to develop the kindness and patience that will result in having a great marriage.

After all, the New Testament tells us in Matthew 19:26, "With men this is impossible, but with God all things are possible." So we must learn to trust God so that He can help us have the kind of marriage He wants us to have.

Looking further at a biblical definition of intimacy—the closeness we are talking about—the Old Testament shares in Genesis 2:25: "And they were both naked, the man and his wife, and were not ashamed." This is much more than physical nakedness—it is emotional, financial, spiritual, and intellectual nakedness.

Being intimate allies, then, means being so emotionally, financially, spiritually, and intellectually connected with your spouse that you are "naked and not ashamed." This concept of nakedness means having nothing between you and your spouse. So being emotionally, financially, spiritually, and intellectually naked means you have nothing to hide from your spouse because you are transparent with each other, which can come only when you have developed a relationship of trust between you. Essentially, this means you have decided to trust each other, which happens only when you each prove to be trust-worthy to the other.

This takes us back to God's intention for marriage, which we find in the New Testament passage of Matthew 19:6, "So then, they are no longer two but one flesh. Therefore, what God has joined together, let not man separate."

The oneness the Bible is speaking about in the passage in Genesis is truly a mystery, in that two individuals—a husband, and a wife—according to the New Testament (1 Corinthians 7:2),[3] join together to form a new identity. And yet, it does not mean that one person becomes subsumed under the personality of the other. Rather, there are two distinct persons, with their own individuality, with their own likes and dislikes, who have chosen to become an "us." So, when one of them hurts, the other one hurts, and when one of them is happy, the other one is also happy, because they have chosen to become intimate allies.

There is hope for today's families only when there is a clear understanding of what is causing the separation and the alienation in marriage so that married people can stay away from that kind of behavior. What we know, based on the marriage research, is that there are barriers to the oneness that needs to take place between a couple in order for them to become intimate allies.

Among the barriers to intimacy we are talking

about are behaviors such as (1) self-protection and the fear of rejection; (2) sin and selfishness; and (3) lack of knowledge.

Because of what many of us experienced while growing up, we tend to self-protect and fear rejection whenever someone has an opinion different from ours. It is a sign of insecurity. This behavior—unfortunately—is very common in marriage. Of course, we've already mentioned the fact that we are all sinners. This reality is at the root of selfishness. We want things to be exactly as we say they should be, because we said so. This makes it difficult to be in an intimate relationship with another human being who may suggest that you do something different from what you want to do. Finally, we simply lack the necessary knowledge to sustain an intimate relationship. We don't know how to communicate effectively. We don't know how to manage conflict. We don't know how to create closeness in our relationships. Hence, becoming intimate allies is impossible when these barriers exist in our marriage relationships.

Becoming intimate allies means embracing the following components in your marriage relationship. First, *oneness*, which is the one flesh experience the Bible speaks about. It is an agreement of emotional, financial, spiritual, intellectual, and physical unity that every successful marriage needs to have. Second, *permanence*, which is the commitment to being married to your spouse until death. It does not mean that God does not love you if you are divorced. God loves you, regardless of your marital state. However, God hates divorce because it separates and hurts people. However, abuse and infidelity also kill permanence in marriage. So, these must be avoided at all cost to enjoy the kind of marriage relation God meant for you to have. Third, *openness*, which means being transparent with your spouse. It is a no-shame relationship. It is an environment of safety and nurture because both husband and wife understand clearly that they are on the same team and have nothing to hide from each other.

Becoming intimate allies is a decision you make to be patient and kind with your spouse and to protect each other from any and every foreign entity that seeks to diminish and destroy your relationship. Being intimate allies is a mindset you nurture every day so that your marriage relationship can be one that brings happiness, fulfillment, and contentment.

This is the kind of marriage relationship we wish for everyone to have.

———————

1. H. Norman Wright, *The Secrets of a Lasting Marriage* (Ventura, CA: Regal Books, 1995), 152.

2. Ellen G. White, *The Adventist Home* (Nashville:

Southern Pub. Assn., 1952), 205.

3. "Nevertheless, because of sexual immorality, let each man have his own wife, and let each woman have her own husband."

6

Communicating
With Grace

People who are intentional about communicating well with their loved ones experience great family relationships. If you think about the people you really like in your family, you would easily admit that the ones you like best are the ones who make you feel good because of the way they speak and listen to you.

A friend of ours told us a story about joining a group of runners from his neighborhood who run five miles every day. After returning from running one day, he was excited about the fact that the second half of the run took less time than the first half. Because he has been concerned about getting back in shape and being healthier, he was feeling good about his improvement in running and mentioned it to his wife when he returned home. Without thinking, she said to him: "The reason you were able to run faster the second half is because most of the trail is downhill on the way back."

Oh my! Our friend felt like someone had punched him in the stomach. Instead of receiving the affirmation he was looking for from his wife—after all the hard work he was putting into his physical exercise—he felt invalidated by the thoughtless response he received from her.

No doubt, people have had much worse things said to them. However, it is fair to ask the question, Did she have to say that? Whether her remarks were correct or not makes no difference. What we know is that nothing positive can come from these types of observations.

If you want your family relationships to be healthy and positive, it is important to learn to communicate with grace.

When we say *grace*, we are talking about the spiritual concept that refers to the unmerited favor and love freely given by God to humans. Grace is something we do not deserve. In the same way God forgives our shortcomings even when we do not deserve to be forgiven, to communicate with grace means to speak with someone in a way they do not deserve.

The Old Testament says in Proverbs 25:11, "A word fitly spoken is like apples of gold in settings of silver."

This is how families can create a life of peace and happiness together, by using words as precious gifts of gold and silver they can give to each other every day, even when a loved one may not deserve it. Can you think of someone in your family with whom you need to use grace in your communication? This is an easy question for most of us to respond to because a large percentage of the world's population have a relative they have a difficult relationship with.

In an earlier chapter, we mentioned the concept presented by Dr. Stephen R. Covey, to "be proactive" for effective communication. This idea encourages people to live within what he calls their "Circle of Control," rather than living in what he calls their "Circle of No Control." When you live in your Circle of Control, you spend most of your time controlling the only person you can really control—yourself. This is the opposite of living most of your life in your Circle of No Control, which is where people spend most of their time trying to control others. People who are proactive live their lives in their Circle of Control and are more likely to communicate with grace than individuals who spend their lives in their Circle of No Control.

The truth is you cannot control your spouse, your children, your siblings, your parents, or your relatives. You truly can control only yourself. So when someone says something to you that is not very nice, rather than using your energy trying to change them, it is much more profitable to use that time developing your response of peace and grace. As we have mentioned before, between what someone says to you and your response, there is a space. So, before you respond, remember to do three things in that space: pause, think, and choose.

When someone says something to us we don't like, we tend to respond quickly and in a similar manner. However, to communicate with grace—to respond in a way they do not deserve—you need to be proactive, to live in your Circle of Control, to *pause*, so that you have time to catch your breath before saying something that will cause equal pain or make things worse. In that space—before your response—you also need to *think* about what you should not say and what you should say to make things better. Finally, you need to *choose* the correct response. The correct response is the one that will calm things down rather than add fuel to the fire. This is what it means to use words as gifts of gold and silver.

Individuals who give little thought to building healthy family relationships live in their Circle of No Control. Rather than making careful choices about how they respond in their conversation with a family member, they blame the other person for starting the fight and feel justified in insulting the other person. These individuals respond in a reactive way rather than choosing to be proactive. They do not take the space between what the other person says and their response and do not consider the consequences and impact their response will have on the relationship. Therefore, they do not pause, they do not think, and they do not make good choices for the health of their relationship with the family member in question.

People often tell us it is too difficult to live being this careful not to hurt the feelings of their loved ones. They say it is not normal. That people simply need to quit being so sensitive. That pain will inevitably happen when we communicate with others.

While in some ways this is true, family relationships as well as other relationships are similar to driving a car. When we get to a red traffic light, we stop. What would feel natural is to keep driving to get to our destination more quickly and without interruptions. However, because we are not the only ones driving on the roads of the cities or towns where we live, we have to be mindful of sharing the road with other drivers who are going in different directions.

Traffic lights are present to help all drivers get to their final destinations safely. If we are patient enough, we all get an opportunity to get to where we are going. If we are not careful to give attention to the traffic lights placed in strategic locations, we will most likely run into other cars, potentially hurting ourselves and others, perhaps even causing a fatal accident because of our lack of attention and concern.

Family relationships are very fragile, and the conversations you have in those relationships need great care. If you are intentional about being careful and nurturing in your family relationships, those choices will help keep your relationships safe and avoid hurt feelings that may lead to the death of a relationship.

So, what is the responsibility of the husband with hurt feelings? Does the fact that his wife said something to cause him pain give him the right to say something to hurt her back? Of course not. In fact, this is his opportunity to communicate with grace. To respond to his wife in a way that she may not deserve. That is the true meaning of grace. Here is where the husband needs to live in his Circle of Control and be proactive. Here is where the husband gets to pause, to think, and to choose the correct response, to keep his marriage relationship healthy and strong, despite what his wife said.

It is true that because we are all human, even if we don't mean to hurt one of our family members on purpose, we will predictably say something or do something that causes them pain. When this happens, it is our opportunity to apologize; this is her opportunity to live in her Circle of Control and take responsibility for what she did rather than blaming the other person for being too sensitive. This is where the wife can say that she is sorry for causing her husband emotional pain, even if that was not her intention. Here is where the wife can decide to pause, think, and choose the correct response to help build a stronger and healthier relationship with her husband.

The wisdom of the New Testament is also very practical and helpful when looking for effective ways to communicate with grace. We shared this with you earlier, and we want to share again what James 1:19 says: "Everyone should be quick to listen, slow to speak and slow to become angry" (NIV).

So while some may be thinking that women or children should be the ones quick to listen and slow to speak, the wise counsel from the Bible is that "*everyone* should be quick to listen, [and] slow to speak." Which means, no one in the family is without responsibility to communicate well, to communicate with grace. And, often, communicating well begins by learning to listen well to enhance all of our family relationships.

7

No Excuse for
Abuse in the Family

In February 2013, people around the world were watching their televisions closely to hear the verdict in the trial of Oscar Pistorius, the famed Paralympic and Olympic Games runner. He was found guilty of shooting to death his girlfriend Reeva Steenkamp; he claimed he mistook her for an intruder in the apartment they shared.

Clearly, we don't have to look far to know that violence has invaded our society, and there are many cases all over the world that will never make the headlines.

Families are being torn apart by senseless violence right in their own homes, as many people choose violence as the primary means of communicating with each other. The impact of these choices is incredibly far-reaching and very destructive to individuals of every age, and also to their families.

While we may not be able to control the violence around us, the good news is that through the power of God, there is an unlimited supply of self-control available to those who request and accept it. God's Word is filled with counsel on how to build healthy, strong relationships, especially in our families.

In this chapter, we will briefly look at the destructive nature of violence and abuse in the family, and we will review God's original intent and perfect plan for our relationships and families. We will also explore the elements of healthy, godly relationships. Many groups all over the world are committed to stopping the violence and preventing violence by providing individuals and families with skills and insights needed to have wholesome relationships.

It is evident from the pervasive incidents of abuse in our homes today that we are far removed from God's ideal for human relationships. Many who profess to be Christians possess none of the characteristics of Christ.

Unfortunately, in too many situations, abusers have misused Scripture and theology to justify their abusive behaviors. In addition, other well-meaning helpers have also misused the Bible to convince victims to accept continued violence in their families. This misuse of Scripture can be dangerous and even lethal to the victims involved. Responsible communities can no longer remain silent.

Silence continues the cycle of domestic violence and does not lead to change. Efforts must be made by every community—especially church communities—to help families stop abuse and assist in creating healthier environments for children, teenagers, and adults.

Of course, it is obvious that we are living in an age of violence. Our senses are bombarded by violence in the news, music, television, and other media outlets. Many people are the target of violence. The victims that most touch our hearts are women and children. It is true that men are also victims of abuse and violence, but in smaller numbers—which may be due to lack of reporting. Regardless of who the victim is, domestic or family violence is incompatible with God's plan for the human family.

Let's first look at some definitions and general information about domestic violence. Domestic violence includes physical abuse, sexual abuse, and emotional abuse. There is no hierarchy of abuse—each one is destructive.

Physical abuse may include behaviors such as pushing and kicking, and it can escalate into more harmful attacks. While it can start with minor bruising, it could end in murder.

Sexual abuse can include inappropriate touching and verbal remarks. Rape, molestation, and incest are also included in this category.

Emotional abuse includes behaviors that consistently degrade or belittle the individual. It can include verbal threats, episodes of rage, obscene language, demands for perfection, and invalidation of character and person. Extreme possessiveness, isolation, and depriving someone of economic resources are all psychologically and emotionally abusive.

There is no real profile of abusers or victims. Both may come from all age groups, ethnic groups, socioeconomic classes, professions, and religious or nonreligious communities. Abuse and violence may take several forms: physical, sexual, or emotional. In the case of the elderly and children, it may also include severe neglect.

The victims

- In the United States of America, one in four women will experience domestic violence, also known as intimate partner violence, during her lifetime.[1]

- Women are more likely than men to be killed by an intimate partner.
- Women between the ages of 20 and 24 are at the greatest risk of becoming victims of domestic violence.[2]
- Every year, one in three female homicide victims is murdered by her current or former partner.[3]

The consequences

- Survivors of domestic violence "face high rates of depression, sleep disturbances," and other emotional distress.[4]
- "Domestic violence contributes to poor health for many survivors."[5]
- "Without help, girls who witness domestic violence are more vulnerable to abuse as teens and adults."[6]
- "Without help, boys who witness domestic violence are far more likely to become abusers of their partners and/or children as adults, thus continuing the cycle of violence in the next generation."[7]
- Most incidents of domestic violence are *never* reported.[8]

In domestic violence, there is always misuse of power. Domestic violence is characterized by fear, control, and harm. One person in the relationship uses coercion or force to control the other person or other family members. The abuse can be physical, sexual, or emotional.

There are several reasons why abusers or batterers may choose to abuse their power:

- He thinks it is his right; that is, part of his role.
- He feels entitled to use force.
- He has learned this behavior in his past.
- He thinks this behavior works.

In most reported cases of abuse the abuser is male. However, abusers can also be female. Abuse has no place in healthy, godly relationships.

Abusers assume they have the right to control all members of their family. The willingness to use violence to accomplish this control is from things that he has learned. From various sources, the abuser has learned that it is appropriate for the person who is bigger and stronger—usually a male—to hit others "for their own good" or because he "loves them."

Abusers learn abusive behavior from various sources, including observing parents and peers, misinterpretation of biblical teachings, and from the media—jokes, cartoons, and movies—that portray control and abuse as a normal part of relationships. And sometimes victims even think they are the cause of the abuse. But this is not true. The behavior of the victim does not cause the abuser's violence. The abuser is in control of the violence; the victim is not.

These facts are not pleasant and remind us of the brokenness of the world we live in. The good news and hope for today's families is that God has not left us alone. The Bible presents the true picture of how human relationships should look. Human beings are created by a loving and relational God who created us to be in relationship with Him first and then with others. Because we are created in His image (Genesis 1:27), all of our relationships should be a reflection of Him and His love. Of course, unlike God, we are not perfect, and because of these imperfections we will struggle in our relationships. Therefore, we must seek God's guidance for grace and strength to be more loving, kind, and patient and to exercise self-control in all of our relationships.

God has provided a way for us to have healthy relationships. We are called to build each other up; this is called empowering. When we empower one another in the family, we build high trust in the relationship. When we misuse power by dominance and coercion, we tear down trust. Trust is the key in the empowering process.

Parents who empower their children and prepare them for responsible interdependence will provide their children with the skills necessary to live as healthy adults and to build and maintain healthy relationships. When parents use unhealthy forms of power and control with children, the children detach from their family and learn negative ways of using power and relating to others.

Empowerment is love in action—a godly characteristic we should imitate. If we are able to practice empowerment in our families, it will revolutionize the view of authority in our homes. Coercion and manipulation are the opposite of empowerment. They are a distortion of what true power is. Empowerment is about mutuality and unity.

God's love and grace gives us the power to empower others. When mutual empowerment occurs among family members, each will grow exponentially in humility and love. Truly, family members will begin to grow more into the likeness of Christ. And His power is promised to us as we seek to have healthy relationships.

Many today find themselves outside of this model of healthy family relationships. In homes where abuse has infiltrated, we encourage you—starting today—to strive toward making your home and relationships abuse free. We beg you to recognize the abuse and to seek counsel and professional help as soon as possible to begin the healing process. This step will bring greater hope to your family today.

1. "Get the Facts and Figures," The National Domestic Violence Hotline, http://www.thehotline.org/resources/statistics/.

2. "Domestic Violence," Bay Area Women's Center, http://bawc-mi.org/site15/index.php/2015-03-30-00-21-30/domestic-violence.

3. Ibid.

4. Ibid.

5. Ibid.

6. Ibid.

7. Ibid.

8. Ibid.

8

How to Prevent Marital Distress and Divorce

Weddings are beautiful, delightful, and blissful occasions. When a couple stands at the altar, holding hands, gazing into each other's eyes, reciting their vows, they are filled with joy and hope. Every couple believes their love is so special and their bond so strong that they will remain together "in sickness and in health" and "for better or worse."

The reality is that most couples will end up on one of three paths: couples who flourish, couples who are conflicted, or couples who quit. In the United States and in many countries of the world, 40 to 50 percent of first-time marriages will eventually end in divorce.[1] What happens to the vows of staying together "until death do us part"? Is it that those making the vows did not take them seriously? Or is there a lack of true understanding of what the vows really mean?

As many couples hear about the high failure rate of marriage, they water down their marriage vows by adjusting the words found in traditional vows. Some vows now say, "as long as we both shall love" instead of "as long as we both shall live." It would appear that some couples are setting their expectations lower just in case they are not able to live up to such a high level of commitment.

It does not take careful observation to realize that marriage, as an institution, has taken a big hit around the world. Everyone knows someone or is related to a couple who has experienced divorce. And in countries where there is no legal divorce, many couples are separated, live separate lives while occupying the same home, or live with high levels of distress. To be sure, most of us have lived through, either firsthand or up close, the pain of strained relationships.

With this daunting reality, how does a couple stay happily married for a lifetime? How does a couple in today's society build a marriage that lasts a lifetime or live "happily ever after"? Is it possible to prevent distress and divorce? Well, the good news is that couples can stay happily married for a lifetime, minimize distress, and stay out of the divorce courts.

Most of us have heard about or have experienced firsthand *falling in love*. At least that is what our society calls it. That giddy, butterflies-in-the-stomach rush of feelings we get when we meet someone we are powerfully attracted to—but this is not really love. Rather, it is just the body's natural response to the neurochemicals that are being pumped into the limbic system of the brain when we meet someone that we find attractive. We prefer to call it *falling in like*.

Another truth is that this giddy response is not sustainable with the same person unless we are intentional about connecting positively on a daily basis. The powerful force that connects us at the beginning begins to wear off once we stop doing all the wonderful things we did at the beginning of the relationship and we have to negotiate the daily cares of life. People have been brainwashed to believe that when the romantic feelings dissolve, they have fallen *out of love*.

Psychologists and other scientists are discovering that humans are wired to intimately connect with another human being. People have the need for trust, safety, and security with someone who is not a part of their family of origin. The opposite of closeness or intimacy is isolation, and our brains interpret this isolation as dangerous to our well-being. That is why getting married is still one of the top goals of most people. Having a life partner is often our only or most reliable source of support, comfort, and intimacy. In this age of growing isolation and loneliness, even scientists agree that now more than ever, people need to be in lifelong committed relationships, and evidence suggests that it is possible to sustain these romantic bonds in a committed relationship like marriage.

The feeling of *falling in love* is a beautiful thing. But relationships are dynamic, and they are always changing. Thus, in spite of how deep this love seems, it is based solely on a feeling and an extremely shallow level of commitment that will eventually fade or dissipate. However, with much effort, time, commitment, and willingness to keep going, it is possible to grow and sustain—or reignite—a love that can be satisfying and stable for a lifetime.

Building a successful marriage is like building a home. It requires a plan and commitment to a lot of hard work. We offer five essential building steps for a strong and healthy marriage.

1. Build your marriage on real love

Real love requires understanding each other's needs and being willing to sometimes practice self-denial for the sake of the relationship. Real love requires much energy and sacrifice but keeps us determined to create the best marriage possible. The New Testament wisdom offers,

> Love is patient and kind; love does not envy or boast; it is not arrogant or rude. It does not insist on its own way; it is not irritable or resentful; it does not rejoice at wrongdoing, but rejoices with the truth. Love bears all things, believes all things, hopes all things, endures all things.
>
> Love never ends. As for prophecies, they will pass away; as for tongues, they will cease; as for knowledge, it will pass away (1 Corinthians 13:4–8, ESV).

2. Accept each other's faults and imperfections

In marriage, we must learn to value each other and accept that we are not perfect. We are talking about having a marriage filled with grace. Grace is something that you give to someone even if they do not deserve it. So you give kindness, patience, gentleness, and more; even when you do not feel like it. Why? Because at some point—even daily—your spouse will have to do the same for you.

The wonderful thing about grace is that you cannot earn it or buy it. And as the giver of grace, you get to offer love and acceptance as a gift to your spouse. Grace in the marriage creates an atmosphere that goes beyond guilt and shame and sets the stage for growth and renewed commitment in the relationship.

3. Listen to each other

A large body of marriage research literature suggests most relationships experience distress because of the lack of effective communication. If married people, and people in general, learned to communicate better, they would have much more understanding between them and a basis for a stronger and healthier relationship.

Good communication in any relationship is like water and sunshine to a healthy lawn. Good listening is like the fertilizer that will go deep beneath the surface to nourish and enrich the soil. In most relationships when there is a complaint, it is because some needs are not being met—voices are not being heard. Couples who communicate well understand that active listening is an essential ingredient in their marriage.

Active listening means listening with your ears, eyes, and heart. It conveys to your spouse that you are more interested in hearing what they have to say than defending yourself and stating your point. Again, active listening necessitates self-denial, another essential ingredient for marriage to last for a lifetime.

When each person in the marriage feels heard and understood, the couple draws closer to each other, intimacy increases, and commitment to one another and the relationship is strengthened.

4. Forgive often

The *Oxford English Dictionary* (1989) has these definitions of *forgiveness*: (1) to stop feeling angry towards (someone) for an offense, flaw, or mistake; (2) to no longer feel angry or wish to punish; (3) to cancel a debt.

Forgiveness paves the way for healing and reconciliation in every relationship. In marriage, both individuals will inevitably hurt each other. When we forgive, we give up our perceived right to punish or retaliate for the wrong that has been done to us. When we fail to forgive, bitterness and resentment increase in the relationship. Forgiveness releases us from these feelings. Forgiveness in essence is for the forgiver more than for the forgiven.

5. Hug more

Most couples can hardly wait to get married to enjoy the physical benefits of marriage. But as daily life takes over and the giddiness wears off, we forget to do the things we did at first.

Hugging is an easy way to reconnect daily. When we hug or touch each other, the hormone oxytocin is released. Oxytocin is the hormone that increases our bond to another person; it also lowers blood pressure and reduces stress. So there are many benefits we can glean from a simple hug. We encourage couples to hug for a minute every morning before parting from each other, and every evening when they are reunited.

Conclusion

What separates successful marriages from those that consistently experience distress or end in divorce are relational skills—knowing how to sustain real love, manage conflict, practice forgiveness and acceptance, maintain romance, and improve communication. Most couples are not adequately prepared for this, but every couple can learn! It is dangerous to become complacent or foster hopelessness in your marriage.

If you are willing to integrate these building steps into your marriage, you will build a marriage that will weather the storms of life. Although all marriages will experience distress at some time or another, they do not need to dissolve when trials come. Couples who learn to work together as a team during good times and bad times will see their marriage not only survive but thrive, and they will "live happily ever after"!

1. "Marriages and Divorces," DivorceStatistics, http:// Divorcestatistics.org; "Crude Divorce Rate," Eurostat, http://ec.europa.eu/eurostat/web/products-datasets/-/ tps00013.

9

Finding Peace
as a Single Person

We recently celebrated thirty-four years of marriage. For some of you, this is longer than you have been alive. However, to us, it seems like it was just yesterday that we were exchanging marriage vows on a lovely summer afternoon in the northeastern part of the United States of America.

As we stood before the minister so long ago, promising to love each other "till death do us part," we had no idea it would be so challenging to keep those vows unbroken. The words were quite easy to say, especially in that atmosphere of ecstasy and anticipation. On the other hand, nothing could have prepared us for the very satisfying life we have experienced as husband and wife, despite having to come to grips with the fact that there are no perfect marriages because there are no perfect people.

Many single adults wish they could be married and believe it would be easier to manage and live responsible lives if this was their reality. Is this really true? Do married people have an advantage in the sex-crazed world that we inhabit? Or are married people also vulnerable, as they have to deal with the pressures of life with its deadlines and demands to succeed?

The truth is, while getting married is relatively easy, staying married is much more difficult. So what is a single person to do until he or she finds the right person to marry, given the very strong sexual urges and ever-present sexual messages that are a reality in postmodern life today?

As we explore this very important topic, it is essential to recognize that sexuality was God's idea, and without a doubt, it is very good. However, everything God has created for your good, the evil one has tried to destroy. Like Eve's experience with the serpent in the Garden of Eden, the evil one continues to present attractive alternatives to God's life-enhancing instructions, hoping you will fall for his lies, leading to grief and suffering in the end.

It was at the very beginning that God declared in Genesis 2:24, 25: "Therefore a man shall leave his father and his mother and hold fast to his wife, and they shall become one flesh. And the man and his wife were both naked and were not ashamed" (ESV). According to the Bible, there is a specific context for sexual expression—after a person leaves father and mother and commits to their spouse. This is the setting in which there is no shame for sexual activity, since it is in this context that a person has taken a pledge of life-long commitment to another human being and is now ready to enjoy the privileges that come with such a devotion.

Just in case you are uncertain about what God is saying, He states, "For this is the will of God, your sanctification: that you abstain from sexual immorality; that each of you know how to con-trol his own body in holiness and honor, not in the passion of lust like the Gentiles who do not know God" (1 Thessalonians 4:3–5, ESV). This passage makes very clear that if you claim to be a believer in God, you are in control of your body and your passions so that you can live a life of moral integrity and honor for God.

The Bible continues to express the appro-priate context for sexual activity by stating in

1 Corinthians 7:1, 2: " 'It is good for a man not to have sexual relations with a woman.' But because of the temptation to sexual immorality, each man should have his own wife and each woman her own husband." To be sure, this inspired counsel is not simply for saints in heaven, but it is established in the reality of life on earth. The Bible writer accepts that because humans are hardwired by God to have sexual intercourse, they will have a deep desire to do so. However, this reality does not give humans who want to live upstanding moral lives—or be obedient to God—license to do away with the principles established by God in the beginning. Instead, the limitations are clear: for sexual expression to take place, it *must* take place between a man and his wife, or a woman and her husband. Please also don't miss the message that if you are male, you are married to a woman, and if you are a woman, you are married to a man.

Walter Trobisch, a German writer on marriage and family issues, once said, "Sex is no test of love, for it is precisely the very thing one wants to test that is destroyed by the testing."[1] This statement is the very opposite to the practices of our day, in which the *individual* is the highest value in society. This means that whatever a person feels like doing, he or she has the right to do, as long as no one is getting hurt in the process. Of course, such a narcissistic and hedonistic person couldn't care less about who is hurt in the process. This type of person is only interested in what they can get rather than what they can give. True love always asks the question, What can I give? rather than What can I get? This concept is documented in the Bible, in John 3:16, which states: "For God so loved the world that *He gave . . .*" (emphasis added).

Taking your chances with the ethics of the God who created you to live a moral and responsible life is without a doubt the better of the two options. In Jeremiah 29:11, God says: "For I know the plans I have for you, declares the LORD, plans for welfare and not for evil, to give you a future and a hope" (ESV). This is a good place to begin when it comes to our sexual ethics of finding peace as a single person.

With regard to a good place to begin, Stephen R. Covey, in his book, *The 7 Habits of Highly Effective Families*, identifies as habit no. 2, begin with the end in mind. This habit is compared to the flight of an airplane. When airplanes travel from one place to another, the pilots have to file a flight plan with a clear destination in mind. This is extremely important, because regularly there are storms that develop during the journey, forcing the pilot to steer the plane over or around the storm. However, because a flight plan was filed with a clear destination in mind, as long as the pilot follows the flight plan, more than likely the plane will land at that final destination close to the time that was planned.

The same is true with your life. You must decide very early in your journey what is the clear destination you want for yourself and for your relationships. Once you have agreed on what kind of life you want to live, you will need to create a mission statement that will keep you focused on the final destination you have chosen for yourself. Your flight plan is like your values. You must decide what values you will embrace as part of your flight and what values you will keep out of your flight plan so that you can arrive safely at the destination you have in mind for your life.

Feelings and urges will undoubtedly develop during your journey, just as storms present themselves in a literal plane flight. However, if the flight plan of your life is filled with the values found in the Bible as your moral compass, you will be more likely to arrive at the destination you chose for yourself at the beginning of your journey.

One of the pitfalls that leads to sexual immorality is a person's thought life. What a person thinks has much to do with what he or she looks at and listens to. Never before in the history of humankind has exposure to looking at and listening to immoral content multiplied as is being experienced today. The internet has made life easier in so many ways for people around the world but at the same time has made being a moral person much more difficult than ever before. With computers, tablets, and smartphones accessible to so many, remaining a morally upright person is becoming more challenging to all. It is also important to accept that single people don't have a corner on this kind of temptation that is an equal-opportunity reality to every human being—married or single. It is the reason the Bible says in Proverbs 4:23, "Above all else, guard your heart, for everything you do flows from it" (NIV).

So, contrary to the established thinking in today's societies, that people cannot do anything about training their sexual drive, it is well documented among scientists that the brain is the most important sex organ humans have. So, human sexuality is worlds apart from "the birds and the bees." The fact is that the sexual drive in humans operates out of the prefrontal cortex of the brain—that part of the brain where all learning takes place and that is the center of judgment. Because God made humans with a brain, they are responsible for their sexuality and the choices they make about it each day. Human beings have the power to make choices, even when their biochemistry battles their brain.

People get to use their highly developed brains to decide how, when, where, and whether they will give expression to their sexual urges. This reality is what separates humans from animals.

Another lie being perpetrated in society today is that having sex will bolster self-image by making you more desirable or more confident. Women, especially, want to be desirable, and often use sex as a barometer of worthiness and as a means to relational connectedness. Men, on the other hand, use sex to make themselves feel more confident and capable; it is really about power and performance, competition and achievement, and for many it is all a numbers game to determine how many conquests they have enjoyed.

Unfortunately, premarital and/or extramarital sex will never validate you or your relationship. If you are a woman, it won't make you more desirable. If you are a man, it won't get rid of your insecurity; in fact, clandestine sex is more likely to have the opposite effect on you. It will end up making you feel more self-denigrated, desperate, alone, and insecure.

So, what is a sexual being to do? There is a need to be aware of the choices you have and handle them instead of allowing them to handle you. Here are a number of those choices now: the "it just happened" choice; the "if we're in love it can't be wrong" choice; the "sex brings us closer together" choice; the "I'm not sexual until I'm married" choice; and the "let's set boundaries" choice. Married or single, all these choices are bogus except for the last choice. Unless you set healthy boundaries ahead of time, whether married or single, you will be in trouble; so, set those healthy boundaries now, before the temptation presents itself.

To find peace as a single person, it is important that you identify your values early, choose to be directed by them, and trust God for the moral strength to live by them each day.

---

1. Walter Trobisch, *I Married You* (New York: Harper and Row, 1971), 75–77.

Afterword

Not long ago we were talking with a couple who had been married for more than twenty-five years, and the wife was blissfully sharing the wonderful vacation they had just enjoyed in Aruba. It was evident she was very excited about the opportunity to share with us that she and her husband had made their marriage such a priority that they had saved funds to enjoy time away together in a beautiful place. No sooner had she mentioned the place where they had vacationed than the husband chimed in, almost annoyed, "No dear," he said, "we went to Barbados, remember?" The bubbly and cheerful demeanor of the lovely lady suddenly changed from joy to sorrow.

On a different occasion, we were speaking to a family with three teenage children, and the youngest son was sharing with a measure of pride that he had learned to water-ski at summer camp three years ago. One could not easily miss how much this youngster enjoyed the activity he was talking about and that he felt pretty confident about the skills he had mastered, when his mother cut into the conversation and said: "It was two years ago, Matthew, not three years ago." The youngster's response was instantaneous. The once-happy face was replaced by a scowl, and confident body language gave way to drooping shoulders.

We share these stories to make the point that we have never experienced couples growing happier in their relationships or a parent-child connection enhanced because the unsolicited help of a family member corrected their story.

The truth is, as kind as the husband was trying to be in the first story, and as helpful as the mother was attempting to be in the second anecdote, these are very offensive examples of the tendency many of us have to correct one another, particularly those who are closest to us, in public. These instances also reveal how ill-mannered and potentially destructive this practice can be to the quality of a relationship.

In both of these illustrations, the correction was completely needless, adding no real value to the information that was being shared. Clearly there was no intent to deceive on the part of the happy wife about where they had been on vacation, since both Aruba and Barbados are beautiful Caribbean islands, with wonderful beaches to enjoy. Neither was there an attempt to deceive on the part of the teen about how long it had been since he learned to water-ski; whether two or three years ago, it surely didn't matter.

So watch out for the habits you have developed and are practicing in your family relationships every day. While it is true that your family members are not perfect and, like you, are apt to make inadvertent errors or forget the exact details of a story, the way you relate to what they are saying will enhance or disrupt your relationship. While their imperfect stories will not hurt anyone, your constant corrections will convey that speaking in your presence may not be safe for them.

A few months ago, we were counseling with a woman who had been married for fifteen years and had two school-age children. She was really upset that her husband was always busy with work and never had time for her or the children. "I don't believe my husband loves me anymore," she said. "I've been waiting for a long time for him to get less busy, but nothing has changed in the last ten years. I am tired of waiting and want out of this miserable marriage," she shared.

On another occasion we spoke with a woman who told us: "Does God expect me to be married to a drug addict? My husband is one, and sometimes I am afraid for my life and that of our children when he becomes violent or buys drugs with the money we need to pay bills."

We felt the profound pain of a young woman we were talking with a few weeks ago when she shared with us: "We have been married for three years, and my husband has already forgotten to be romantic. What can I say to him or do to encourage him to do a better job of staying romantic?"

While women tend to seek us out more often than men to talk about their relationships, we could feel his deep burden when the man we were speaking with a few months ago told us: "My wife is simply impossible to live with. Every time we have a conversation about anything that is significant, it ends up in a fight because she *must* have it her way. It really doesn't matter what the situation is, the pattern is the same. I always feel invalidated when I talk with my wife about anything because she is always right and I am always wrong. As the man in this relationship, I am of the impression that God expects me to be the leader. But with a woman like my wife, I don't believe it is possible to accomplish God's purposes in our marriage. I am tired and frustrated and don't know what to do anymore."

As we said at the beginning of this book, marriage and family relationships are the most challenging experiences human beings can have. And, it is true that there are no perfect families because there are no perfect people.

It is our hope that as you make relationship choices for your life in the days ahead regardless of your status—married, divorced, widowed, never married, younger, middle-aged, or older— you will do so with the confidence that you are not alone in your quest for greater peace and happiness.

Despite the fact that healthy family relationships are difficult to develop and sustain, more than ever we believe and are encouraged that there is hope for today's families. And yet the hope is not only in the counsel we have shared in these pages about the choices you can make to respond in a better way: to be proactive, to pause, to think, and to choose the correct response in your interactions with loved ones. The hope is not only in the fact that you can seek help from professional counselors who can assist you to gain perspective and process ways to learn better skills for building stronger relationships. The hope is not only in the fact that you can remember to make deposits in the emotional bank accounts of your family members each day. The real hope is in the promises of God to help you in situations that seem impossible when He states in Mark 10:27, "With man it is impossible, but not with God. For all things are possible with God" (ESV).

To have God on your side is very significant. Seek Him in your journey through life, look to Him when you face decisions. In fact, He wants to have a part in your life: He wants to speak to you when you read His Word; as you talk to Him in prayer. The best decision you can make for your family is to make God the third column in your marriage—the Counselor and Guide for you and your children, a real source of hope when everything around you seems hopeless.

This is His invitation to you and your loved ones: "Behold, I stand at the door and knock. If anyone hears My voice and opens the door, I will come in to him and dine with him, and he with Me" (Revelation 3:20). Will you give Him a chance?

This is our hope for your family relationships. More than hope so, we pray so.

FREE Lessons at www.BibleStudies.com

Call:
1-888-456-7933

Write:
Discover
P.O. Box 999
Loveland, CO 80539-0999

It's easy to learn more about the Bible!

SHARING HOPE

Download our app today
and start reading
more books like
Hope for Today's Families!

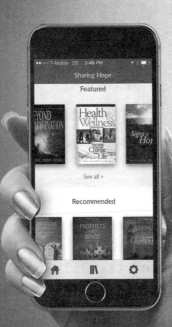